W9-CTO-649

...ABITS

Exercise

Jayne Denshire

This edition first published in 2011 in the United States of America by Smart Apple Media. All rights reserved. No part of this book may be reproduced in any form or by any means without written permission from the publisher.

Smart Apple Media
P.O. Box 3263
Mankato, MN, 56002

First published in 2010 by
MACMILLAN EDUCATION AUSTRALIA PTY LTD
15–19 Claremont St, South Yarra, Australia 3141

Visit our web site at www.macmillan.com.au or go directly to www.macmillanlibrary.com.au

Associated companies and representatives throughout the world.

Copyright © Jayne Denshire 2010

Library of Congress Cataloging-in-Publication Data

Denshire, Jayne.
Exercise / Jayne Denshire.
      p. cm. — (Healthy habits)
Includes index.
ISBN 978-1-59920-547-2 (library binding)
1. Exercise—Juvenile literature. I. Title.
RA781.D443 2011
613—dc22
                                    2009038469

Edited by Helena Newton
Text and cover design by Kerri Wilson
Page layout by Domenic Lauricella
Photo research by Jes Senbergs
Illustrations by Richard Morden

Manufactured in China by Macmillan Production (Asia) Ltd.
Kwun Tong, Kowloon, Hong Kong
Supplier Code: CP December 2009

Acknowledgments
The author and the publisher are grateful to the following for permission to reproduce copyright material:

Front cover photograph: Two children playing soccer courtesy of iStockphoto

© Olivia Baumgartner/Sygma/Corbis, **7** (middle); Dreamstime/D.T Guy, **16**; Getty Images, **14**; Adrian Dennis/AFP/Getty Images, **23**; J. Clarke/Getty Images, **24**; David Madison/Getty Images, **10**; Jose Luis Pelaez/Getty Images, **11**; Riccardo Savi/Getty Images, **15**; Taxi/Getty Images, **9**; iStockphoto, **1**, **6** (top); © Rob Friedman/iStockphoto, **3**, **19**; © Kim Gunkel/iStockphoto, **7** (bottom); © Juan Monino/iStockphoto, **7** (top); © Glenda Powers/iStockphoto, **6** (bottom); Jupiter Images, **6** (middle), **8**, **20**, **25** (top), **26**; Newspix/News Ltd/Watt Michael, **18**; Photolibrary © Bubbles Photolibrary/Alamy, **21**; Photolibrary © Ulrich Doering/ Alamy, **22**; Photolibrary © Imagebroker/Alamy, **5**; Photolibrary © Jeff Morgan Education/Alamy, **25** (bottom); Photolibrary © James Schwabel/Alamy, **12**; Photolibrary/Gabe Palmer, **17**; © Sonya Etchison/Shutterstock, **13**; © Monkey Business Images/ Shutterstock, **4**.

While every care has been taken to trace and acknowledge copyright, the publisher tenders their apologies for any accidental infringement where copyright has proved untraceable. Where the attempt has been unsuccessful, the publisher welcomes information that would redress the situation.

Contents

When a word is printed in **bold**, you can look up its meaning in the Glossary on page 31.

Healthy Habits

Healthy habits are actions we learn and understandings we develop. These actions and understandings help us be happy and healthy human beings.

Getting out in the fresh air is a healthy habit we can all learn.

If we do something often, we can carry out the action without thinking about it. This action is called a habit.

Putting on a hat every time you go out in the sun is a healthy habit.

Developing Healthy Habits

If we develop healthy habits when we are young, they become good choices for life. We can develop healthy habits in these six ways.

1 Exercise
Good exercise habits keep us fit and healthy.

2 Hygiene
Good **hygiene** habits keep us clean and healthy.

3 Nutrition
Good **nutrition** habits keep us growing and healthy.

4 Rest and sleep
Good rest and sleep habits keep us relaxed, energetic, and healthy.

5 Safety
Good safety habits keep us safe and healthy.

6 Well-being
Good **well-being** habits keep us feeling happy and healthy.

What Is Exercise?

Exercise is any activity that moves your body to keep you fit and healthy. Exercise uses your muscles and gets your heart pumping blood around your body.

Running with friends in the park is healthy exercise.

Exercise is an important habit to develop when you are young. This will make it easier to keep exercise a healthy habit throughout your life.

Walking for exercise is a healthy habit you can develop at a young age.

Why Should You Exercise?

Exercise makes your muscles stronger and keeps your bones healthy. It helps keep your weight healthy and helps prevent **disease**. Exercise also helps you think more clearly.

Playing tennis makes your muscles stronger and helps you move your arms and legs better.

Your body was made to move. If you sit still a lot, some parts of your body do not get used enough. Exercise gets your body moving.

Sitting at the computer for a long time can make your muscles stiff.

Types of Exercise

Some types of exercise make your heart and lungs work harder when you do them. These are called aerobic exercise. Aerobic means "with **oxygen**."

Running is an aerobic exercise, because your heart and lungs work harder when you run.

Other types of exercise build up your muscle strength. These are called anaerobic exercise. Anaerobic means "without oxygen."

Swinging on a bar is an anaerobic exercise, because you use your muscles to do it.

Exercise Tips

Remember these tips when you exercise:
- Warm up your muscles by stretching before you start.
- Cool down your muscles by stretching after you finish.
- Drink plenty of water.

Stretching before you start to exercise will help prevent injuries while you are exercising.

What to Wear

It is best to wear comfortable clothes and shoes when you exercise. You may need to wear special clothing for certain types of exercise.

Exercise clothing is often made from material that allows sweat to dry quickly.

loose-fitting shirt

comfortable shorts

socks that cushion your feet and absorb sweat

shoes that fit well

Exercise on Your Own

You can do many exercise activities on your own. These include walking, swimming, skating, and gymnastics.

Walking makes your leg muscles strong and improves your aerobic fitness.

Gymnastics

Gymnastics is a set of exercises you perform. These exercises help make you strong and **agile.** You may need special equipment for gymnastics, such as a balance beam.

Gymnastics improves your body's balance and strength.

Exercise with Others

When you exercise with others, you are usually part of a team. Training and playing with others helps you learn teamwork skills while you exercise.

Hockey is a team sport that makes your legs and arms strong.

Basketball

Basketball is a team sport with five team members on the court at a time. To play basketball, you need to be able to run, jump, throw, and catch.

basketball, you run up and down the court, which improves our aerobic fitness.

Being Fit

Being fit means you can do more activity using less energy. When you are fit, your **stamina** increases and you can do more without feeling tired.

Skipping builds stamina makes your heart stronger, and helps you lungs work better.

Your Pulse

Your pulse is the speed at which your heart pumps blood. Each count in your pulse comes from a **heartbeat**. Your pulse gets faster when you exercise.

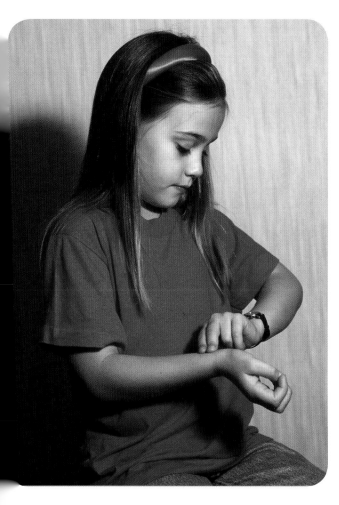

You can measure your pulse by counting how often your blood pumps in your wrist.

Exercise Competitions

Sometimes people enter exercise competitions. Students often compete to win events at school swimming and **athletic** meets.

There are local clubs you can join to compete in exercise competitions, such as swimming.

Athletes from around the world compete with each other at the Olympic Games. These athletes are the best in the world at their chosen type of exercise.

Javelin is one of the many different events at the Olympic Games.

People Who Help Us with Exercise

Some people have jobs in exercise. Coaches, personal trainers, and gym teachers all work to help us with exercise.

Coaches teach people how to play their sport better. They give players practice in the skills needed for their sport. They also help improve players' fitness for a game or competition.

Personal trainers work with people to improve their fitness. They take people through activities that help with their muscle strength, stamina, and general health.

Gym teachers run school physical education programs. They teach students activities such as gymnastics and ball skills. They also arrange for students to play team sports, sometimes against other schools.

Make Exercise a Healthy Habit

Making exercise a healthy habit means finding time for exercise in your life. Getting regular exercise is important to keep you healthy and strong.

Taking part in a sports event whenever you can is a great healthy exercise habit.

Healthy Exercise Checklist

This checklist shows how often you should do these healthy exercise habits.

Healthy Exercise Habit	every time you exercise	every two or three weeks	every few months	whenever you can
stretch before you exercise	✔			
try a new team sport			✔	
take part in a sports event				✔
practice ball skills		✔		
try a new type of exercise			✔	
cool down after exercise	✔			
drink water when you exercise	✔			

Try This Healthy Habit!

You can create a fitness course on your own or with friends. Set it up in a clear space, and use whatever equipment you can find.

What You Need:
- five pieces of paper or card, numbered 1 to 5
- five small cups of water for each person

Suggested Equipment:
- lengths of colored ribbon to swirl around
- jump rope for skipping with
- ball for throwing or bouncing
- some steps to step up and down

You can ask a parent for help.

What To Do:

1 Set up five activities in your fitness circuit. Decide what each activity will involve, such as bouncing a basketball or skipping.

2 Place a number at each activity.

3 Place one cup of water for each person near each activity.

4 Have each person take his or her pulse, counting the number of beats in the wrist, and record the result.

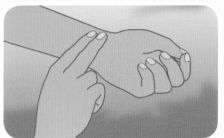

5 Take turns trying each activity for 15 seconds. Take a few sips of water after each one.

Now have each person take his or her pulse again to see if it has changed.

Amazing Exercise Facts

If you walk for one minute, you use 2,500 to 3,500 **calories**. If you run for one minute, you use 7,000 to 9,500 calories.

You sit on your largest muscle! It is called the gluteus maximus, and it is in your bottom.

Aerobic exercise helps make the muscles you use for breathing stronger.

About one-third of what you weigh is muscle.

There are 1,440 minutes in a day. If you move for 60 of them each day, you will keep your body fit.

When exercising, athletes' hearts pump eight times more blood per minute than when resting.

Glossary

agile	move quickly or nimbly
athletes	people trained in sporting or exercise activities
athletics	exercises such as running, jumping, and throwing
calories	units for measuring the energy we get from food
disease	an illness or sickness
heartbeat	a single beat that is felt as a pulse each time blood is pumped through the heart
hygiene	what we do to keep ourselves clean and healthy
nutrition	what our bodies take in and use from the food we eat
oxygen	a gas in the air that living things need to breathe
stamina	being able to exercise for longer periods, using less energy
well-being	a state of feeling healthy and happy

Index